A Self Care Journal

Falling In Love With Yourself

Rose Cushing

A Self Care Journal

Falling In Love With Yourself

Rose Cushing

I want to dedicate this book to the girls in my life. Heather, Ginny, Jen, Amber, Nichole, Kaitlyn, La'Niya, Holly, Elizabeth, Stella and Alasia! May you all know you are loved, valued and strong. The world is yours, you can do anything! I love you.

Copyright 2025 Rose Cushing
ISBN: 978-1-963661-51-4
Cushing Publishing
9380 Driver Road
Middlesex, NC 27557

As women, we so often put selfcare on the back burner, like it is the least important of our responsibilities. At least I know I do.

I designed this journal to help us get in the habit of putting priorities on ourselves, as much as we do for the people we love, the people we work for and care for. We all deserve that.

I want you to reconnect with your feelings, your dreams, your personal goals, and be able to decide your future. Often we forget that we hold the keys to our own destiny. If you don't have the life you really want, well let's get started on making that a reality.

We go through seasons in our life. When we are young and falling in love, learning who we are, and where we are going it is easy to get lost. This journal will give you an opportunity to record your dreams, your feelings, and your thoughts. You will be surprised how much this will help you along your journey. Remember anything is possible!

Later, when we have taken a path for our lives, it often isn't based on our dreams, but what we feel like is reality. I get it. Mine was too. At this stage of your life a journal can be such a great boost for us as our lives revolve around kids, their school, and our family. Don't ever loose sight of who you are, your ideas, your plans. Self-acceptance is so important and part of that is realizing that the things you thought and wanted when you were younger, could have changed drastically as you age.

Then as our kids grow up we begin to have some time to rediscover ourselves, our passions, and to love ourselves for who we are. The journal is a great resource for helping us record our ideas and dreams and figure out which way we truly want to go.

Then in the next season our kids have kids. We are aging, but that doesn't mean that we don't still wish to chase new dreams, new ideas and new ways to love and accept ourselves. You are never to old to start something new.

So I have designed a journaling routine for this journey. Use it daily and I think you will learn to enjoy this journey called life and all the crazy twists and turns it gives us. Fall in love with you again.

So are you ready to get to know yourself again?

THE BEST PROJECT YOU WILL EVER WORK ON IS YOU!

Do you take time for yourself?

_____

_____

_____

When? How?

_____

_____

_____

_____

_____

_____

_____

STOP THE NEGATIVE SELF-TALK

Did you know that we become what we think we are? If you are in a habit of negative talk about yourself, it is very important that you squash that habit today!

READ THAT AGAIN.......What we think, we become. It is a proven fact that negative talk affects us and our self-esteem. Don't be your worst enemy.

Negative talk becomes a bad habit quickly and breaking it is tough. I know you can do it! You just have to be aware of how bad it is for you and change the way you think. We got this.

Remember be gentle with yourself. Talk to yourself as if you were talking to one of your sweet children or grandchildren.

Let's begin.....

What season of life are you currently in?

_____

_____

_____

Do you talk negatively about yourself? Why?

What are your current concerns with where your life is?

_____

_____

_____

_____

_____

_____

What steps are you taking to address those concerns and make positive changes?

_____

_____

_____

_____

_____

_____

Change never happens till we acknowledge the obstacles and address the issues. You got this!

What are three things I like about myself?

_____

_____

_____

_____

_____

What would you like to change about yourself?

_____

_____

_____

_____

_____

Live Simply
Dream Big
Be Grateful
Give Love
Laugh Lots

List 3 things you are grateful for:

_____

_____

_____

Gratitude is noticing and acknowledging the goodness, positives, and blessings in our lives. Gratitude is acknowledges that we have benefited from someone's kindness. Gratitude implies humility in understanding that others have contributed to who we are or where we are in our lives – that we are beneficiaries of kindness, goodness, or positivity.

BE GRATEFUL
for every second of every day that you get to spend with the people you love. Life is so very precious.

How do you show love and affection to yourself?

_____

_____

_____

Showing ourselves love and appreciation is not an act of arrogance or selfishness. It is important to give ourselves credit for the things we accomplish. Everyone likes to hear a "well done" why should we be different in how we treat everyone else?
Celebrate the small victories because they add up to how we view ourselves. Love your self! You are worth it!

Thoughts?

_____

_____

_____

_____

_____

_____

_____

_____

_____

_____

_____

_____

_____

Now that we have listed a couple of things we are grateful for, we have to ask ourselves

What have I shared with or contributed to others?

_____

_____

_____

_____

_____

_____

_____

_____

Tip your server.
Return your shopping cart. Pick up a piece
of trash. Hold the door for the person
behind you.
Let someone into your lane. Small acts can
have a ripple effect.
That's how we change the world.

What are some of your core values?

_____

_____

_____

_____

INTEGRITY IS CHOOSING COURAGE OVER COMFORT. CHOOSING WHAT IS RIGHT OVER WHAT IS FUN, FAST, OR EASY AND CHOOSING TO PRACTICE OUR VALUES RATHER THAN SIMPLY PROFESSING THEM

The Biggest Wall You Must Climb Is The One You Build In Your Mind.

What are your biggest fears and how do they hold you back?

_____

_____

_____

How are you turning those fears into positive lessons ?

_____

_____

_____

—
_____

_____

_____

What would you change if you could?

_____

_____

_____

_____

_____

What are some things you Appreciate about yourself?

_____

_____

_____

What are some things you would change about yourself if you could?

_____

_____

_____

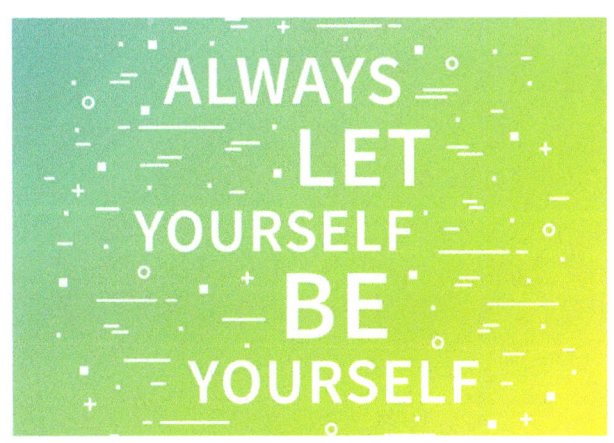

Find Joy In Small Things

What are some of the things that bring you joy?

_____

_____

_____

Living Simply With Intention

When I first started this journey, I had never heard of the idea of living in the moment or intentional living. I must say I was surprised that I didn't know it, and that it was such a powerful thing to include in my life once I understood it.

If you think about it as if your being was in four separate pieces. Your Soul, Mind, Body and your Heart. Each day you need to take a moment to acknowledge each part of your being.

When you focus on your soul, just take a moment to breathe and be.

When you focus on your heart, be thankful for the love you have in your life. Always make sure that you give out much more love than you receive. Paying it forward is always a good idea.

Now take a moment and acknowledge your body. Stretch, reach, extend and move. Be mindful about what you choose to put in your body. The old saying "you are what you eat," is true.

Last, but certainly not least is your mind. Take time to learn something new, change how you think by looking at different points of view. Think your thoughts with care. Remember negativity attracts negativity. Always keep positive, happy thoughts.

If you practice this each day you will know where you are going and be able to embrace and commit to it fully. Success will be yours and congratulate yourself for small wins. They are
 important.

What are some of the ways you live Simply?

_____

_____

_____

_____

_____

_____

_____

_____

_____

_____

_____

Thoughts?

What does living with Intention mean to you?

_____

_____

_____

_____

_____

_____

_____

_____

_____

_____

_____

_____

_____

What are some of the things that you want to accomplish
in your life?

–
_____

_____

_____

_____

What do you dream about?

-
_____

_____

_____

-
_____

_____

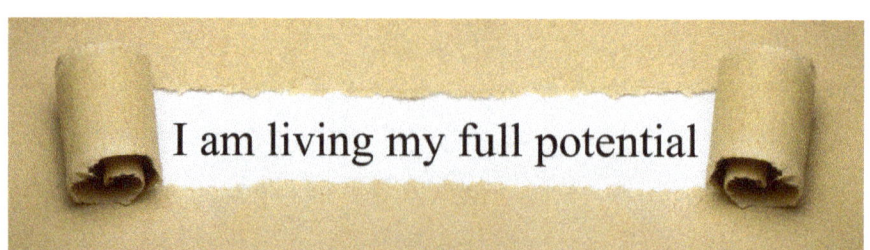

I am living my full potential

Maybe the journey
isn't so much about
becoming anything.
Maybe its about
Un-Becoming every-
thing that isn't really
you! So you can be
who you ere meant to
be in the first place!

Paulo Coelho

What are you letting go to "Un-become"

_____

_____

_____

-
_____

_____

_____

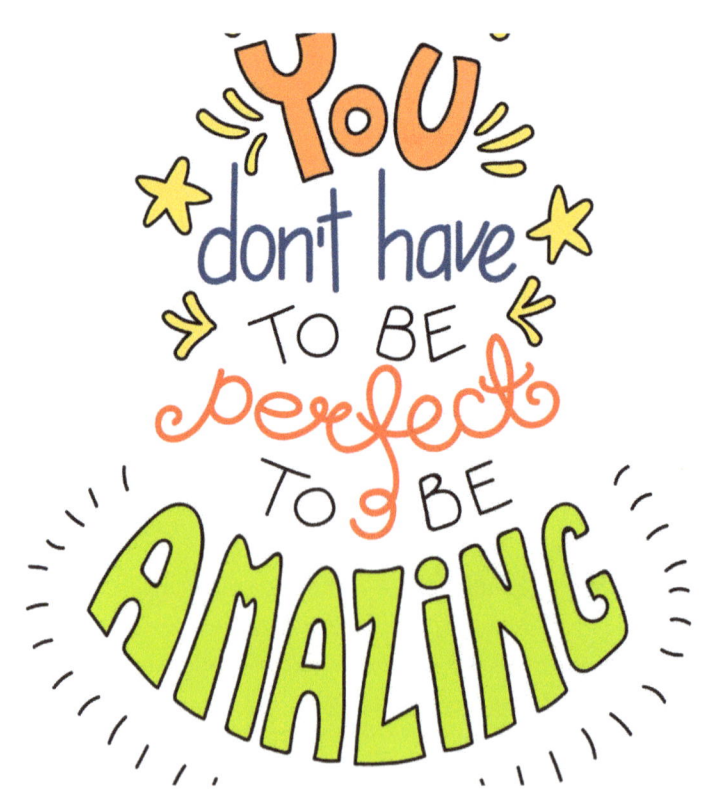

Are you Hopeful about your life?

_____

_____

_____

_____

_____

_____

_____

_____

Do you take risks? Talk about them.

_____

_____

_____

_____

_____

_____

_____

_____

_____

_____

_____

_____

What steps are you taking to achieve your goals?

_____

_____

_____

_____

_____

_____

SUCCESS WILL NOT COME TOMORROW **UNLESS** YOU START **TODAY**

Do you BELIEVE in yourself? Be honest.

_____

_____

_____

_____

_____

_____

_____

_____

_____

_____

_____

List something you are proud of yourself for:

\-
_____

_____

\-
_____

_____

_____

I am proud of you for getting this far! These are tough questions that you have to think about. If you didn't answer each question, you can always go back and fill it in or change it. This is about getting to know you again.

So let's talk about a routine to initiate daily self care.

Bedtime ritual:
1) The single most important thing, I think you can do for yourself, is insure a good night's sleep! I have wrestled with that for many years. So here are some suggestions I have found work to make that happen. Pick a specific time to try to go to bed every night. Teaching ourselves to adhere to a "bedtime" isn't easy, but it is a great help. I chose an activity that I love, but think of it as a "guilty pleasure. Reading, whether it is a current magazine, a book or something to make myself better. I go to bed, select some very calming music and read for about 30 minutes. That is "My time". I take a few moments to say my prayers. (This is important to me)
Then I get organic castor oil from Halfmoonfarms.net. I drop 2-4 drops into my navel to penetrate for better health. (Info on website)

Afterwards, I use Beef Tallow Moisturizer
Butter with Magnesium and Calendula (available at Halfmoon-Farms.net) to my face and to the soles of my feet. (Info on website about why)

Put away all the distractions, focus on the
calming sounds, breath in rhythm and feel your chest rise and fall with the breaths. Close your eyes and drift into sleep.

When I get up in the morning, I thank God for allowing me another day. I make entries in my gratitude journal, look at my daily to-do list and
get ready for a brand new day. Eat breakfast, take my medicines and get in 2000 steps on my eliptical (mine has a motor).

What is your Bedtime routine?

-
_____

_____

_____

-
_____

_____

_____

-
_____

_____

My day begins and ends with gratitude.

What is your morning routine?

_____

_____

_____

_____

_____

_____

_____

_____

_____

_____

_____

_____

How much time do you routinely spend in nature?

Being outside in the sunshine with trees, flowers, and birds is a significant factor in your physical and mental health. Adults need a minimum of 30 minutes per day. The sunshine gives us Vitamin D and the interaction with nature is a significant factor in our mental and physical well being. I always thought bird watching was sort of an old people's thing. But, I am smarter now and I have found that taking time to watch the birds is extremely pleasurable. Taking that time to listen to them sing, watch them fly around the feeder and talk is incredibly relaxing! Nature rebuilds our soul.

_____

_____

_____

What do you enjoy doing?

_____

_____

_____

_____

In this crazy world we live in we lose touch with our roots in nature. We don't take time to stop and appreciate simple pleasures like beautiful trees, the wind whispering through their leaves or the sounds around us. We actually tune them out because they don't fit in with what we expect to hear. Often being replaced by text message notifications, cell phones ringing or buzzing and traffic noise. Have you ever heard of the Japanese solution for stress called Shinrin Yoku or Forest Bathing? I am sure you are thinking forest bathing. What is that?

In Japanese, Shinrin means forest and Yoku means bath. It is a practice for relaxation. A very simple practice to bring calm and peace to your life. It has been proven to lower blood pressure, and reduce stress, along with many other health benefits. It is a simple practice that anyone at any fitness level can do. It is not hiking, jogging, or any type of physical exercise. It is simply being in nature and being still, quieting our minds.

Find a spot that appeals to you. It can be a nearby park, a beach, or just a walk in the woods. Turn off all of your electronic devices to become unplugged for a bit. Allow time to slow down around you. There is no schedule to meet, no phone to answer, and nothing but time to soak up and enjoy the surroundings.

Use your five senses. First, let's talk about touch. Rub your hands across the bark of a tree. Feel its texture. Is it rough, or is it smooth? How does it differ from the trees around it or are they all the same? Touch the leaves are they soft or are they a harder texture? Maybe they are pine needles. How do they feel? Take off your shoes and walk barefoot. Allow the soles of your feet to experience the textures of the ground beneath. If there is a stream running through dip your fingers or toes in the water. How does it feel?

Next, let's talk about smell. Begin with deep breathing. What does the tree smell like? Can you catch the smell? What does the air around you smell like? Perhaps you catch a whiff in the air of a blooming flower or vine. Maybe someone nearby is cooking or burning trash. What do you smell?
What do you see? Do you like a particular tree or plant that is in your

surroundings? Maybe it is the fixtures or the historical markers in the park that are appealing. Take note of all the different shades of green that surround you. How the light filters through the tree limbs at different times of the day. Take a moment to reflect on them, what do they mean to you? Do you see other people? Are their animals in the park? Sometimes we are lucky to see squirrels or birds.

What do you hear? Close your eyes and listen for a bit. Do you hear birds singing? Can you identify which ones they are? Maybe children playing nearby, and you hear their laughter. Do you hear the leaves rustling under your feet? If there is a stream, do you hear it flowing? Do these sounds bring back memories from your life? Take a few minutes to reflect on those memories.

Now your sense of taste. Can you taste the fresh spring air on your lips? Do the signs and sounds bring back memories that you can taste?

Taking this time to have a "time out" from the world will do you an immense amount of good. We are so heavily bombarded daily with news, appointments, work, stress, and family that we often overlook our self-care. This exercise done regularly will become something you look forward to and find yourself making time to experience it.

Statistics show that used on a regular basis the art of Shinrin Yoku actually lowers blood pressure, promotes better sleeping and overall improves our health. While relatively unknow here in the states the practice is quite common in the Orient and Europe.

Used for 20 minutes a day several times per week can change your life, literally. This time for personal reflection will benefit you physically, emotionally, and spiritually. This is not just a walk in the woods. For this exercise, you should be completely submersed in your surroundings. Block out all the thoughts of the day and enjoy this experience. Enjoy utilizing all five senses and you will find a sixth sense called "state of mind". I hope you will give it a try and revel in this peace you have found.

How do you "recharge"?

Thoughts?

_____

_____

_____

_____

_____

_____

_____

_____

_____

_____

_____

_____

Meditation

How do you meditate is a question I am often asked. When you look at it on line or out in the world it looks like a very complicated thing that takes a lot of time. So first let's figure out what it is.

Meditation is a practice where an you use a technique such as mindfulness, or focusing the mind on a particular object thought or activity to train attention and awareness. You can achieve a mentally clear and emotionally calm and stable state. Meditation has great benefits such as lowering stress, reducing asthma episodes, physical pain, insomnia, episodic anger, negative or irrational thinking and anxiety. It can also help you learn to cope and focus on a feeling of well being.

Meditation allows you to confront stress, awareness and cope with issues rather than stuffing them in a box for later. It is a very empowering tool. Regular meditation, even a few minutes a day is very beneficial.

Being mindful helps you reduce addiction to drugs, alcohol, shopping and feelings that cause stress and chronic pain. The act of being present makes a great difference in how we approach our life. It also embodies kindness and compassion for yourself.

When my son was in Tae Kwon Do, each day they began with a 5 minute meditation to focus on their exercises for the day. I used to do it with them and focus on my work, problems, self, etc. All you have to do is close your eyes, get in a comfortable position and chase all the thoughts out of your mind. After clearing your mind focus on the moment, the issue, you.

If you visualize it you can achieve it. It really helped me as I began to feel very relaxed and notice that my mind became much clearer about whatever issue it was. Chasing out all the "noise" and focusing on the issue taught me a lot. Just 5 min a day does wonders. In my practice of meditation it has nothing to do with religion of any kind. Just making me a better person.

Live each moment with open heart, presence, clarity and awareness!

Do you meditate?

_____

_____

_____

Meditation can be a very useful tool in allowing us to focus on the things that we want to happen. It also helps us clear our minds and rest our brains from all the influx of information we receive in today's world.

Keep a journal to record your thoughts, ideas and dreams. Begin here

_____

_____

_____

_____

_____

_____

_____

_____

_____

_____

_____

_____

Keep a journal to record your thoughts, ideas and dreams.

_____

_____

_____

_____

_____

_____

_____

_____

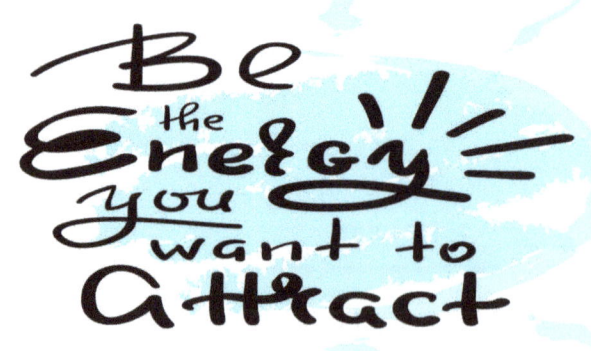

Keep a journal to record your thoughts, ideas and dreams.

_____

_____

_____

_____

_____

_____

_____

_____

Keep a journal to record your thoughts, ideas and dreams.

_____

_____

_____

_____

_____

_____

_____

_____

_____

_____

_____

_____

_____

Keep a journal to record your thoughts, ideas and dreams.

_____

_____

_____

_____

_____

_____

_____

_____

_____

_____

_____

_____

Keep a journal to record your thoughts,
ideas and dreams.

Keep a journal to record your thoughts, ideas and dreams.

_____

_____

_____

_____

_____

_____

_____

_____

_____

_____

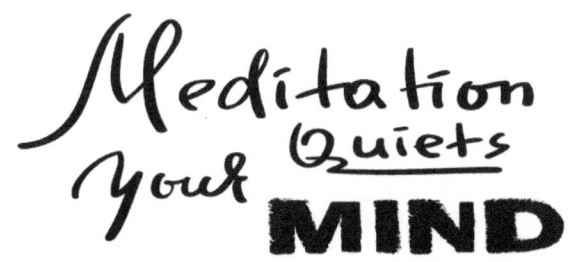

What new dreams are you dreaming since
reading this far?

_____

_____

_____

_____

_____

_____

_____

_____

If you could design yourself as a person what would you look like?

_____

_____

_____

_____

_____

_____

_____

_____

How does that differ from how you look now?

_____

_____

_____

_____

_____

_____

_____

_____

_____

_____

_____

Do you want to add to your educational accomplishments, finish that degree, etc.?

_____

_____

_____

_____

_____

_____

_____

What do you need to change to get your dream job? Education, location?

_____

_____

_____

_____

_____

_____

_____

_____

_____

_____

_____

What is your career now?

_____

_____

_____

_____

_____

_____

_____

_____

_____

_____

_____

_____

What would your career be?

_____

_____

_____

_____

_____

_____

_____

_____

Thoughts?

_____

_____

_____

_____

_____

_____

_____

_____

Thoughts?

_____

_____

_____

_____

_____

_____

_____

_____

_____

_____

_____

_____

Thoughts?

_____

_____

_____

_____

_____

_____

_____

_____

_____

_____

_____

_____

Thoughts?

_____

_____

_____

_____

_____

_____

_____

_____

Thoughts?

_____

_____

_____

_____

_____

_____

_____

_____

Thoughts?

_____

_____

_____

_____

_____

_____

_____

_____

_____

_____

_____

_____

_____

Where do you find inspiration?

_____

_____

_____

_____

_____

_____

_____

_____

_____

_____

_____

_____

_____

How do you add this into your life?

Are you currently working on any projects?

How to you satisfy your creative ideas and dreams?

_____

_____

_____

_____

_____

_____

_____

_____

Journal entries

Journal entries

_____

_____

_____

_____

_____

_____

_____

_____

_____

_____

_____

_____

Journal entries

_____

_____

_____

_____

_____

_____

_____

_____

Journal Entries

_____

_____

_____

_____

_____

_____

_____

_____

_____

_____

_____

_____

I hope that you have found this journal helpful in remembering how awesome you are! Because you are. It's so easy to forget about ourselves as we become bogged down by everything else in the world. Always remember:

1) You are worth every ounce of energy that you put into you.

2) Anything is possible, the world is wide open and waiting for you.

3) Whatever you do for others as a paying it forward will come back to you in so many ways. So take the time to be kind not only to others, but to   yourself.

4) Follow me on Facebook, YouTube and online at www.HalfMoonFarms.net, www.RoseCushing.com

Look for additionial journals coming soon.

Rose

About the Author:

Rose Cushing is an author, podcast host, publisher, television producer home-steader, and documentary film maker. She loves horses, writing, marketing, and gardening.

She also established Cushing Publishing, a small traditional publishing house in 2023. www.CushingPublishing.com Podcasts include Carolina Writers Speak and Today's Horsewoman. These air on all major podcast channels.

After her experience with Fibromyalgia, Rose developed a line of chemical free body, cleaning and household products from her farm, Half Moon Farms. Not stopping there she wanted to write and teach women to love themselves, have the life they desire and find their purpose. Finding your purpose is one of the best things you can do for yourself. Follow these journals, put in the time and you will find your purpose too.